Original title:
In the Heart of the Islands

Copyright © 2025 Creative Arts Management OÜ
All rights reserved.

Author: Elias Montgomery
ISBN HARDBACK: 978-1-80581-534-1
ISBN PAPERBACK: 978-1-80581-061-2
ISBN EBOOK: 978-1-80581-534-1

Where the Sky Kisses the Sea

Seagulls steal fries from my plate,
While the sun dangles on the gate.
Fish wear sunglasses, trying to tan,
And a crab's doing the conga—what a plan!

Waves giggle as they splash and play,
Tickling toes, oh what a day!
A coconut falls—who's at fault?
Guess I'll blame it on the local salt.

A Symphony of Echoing Waves

The ocean sings a silly tune,
While turtles race by, oh so soon.
A mermaid's lost her favorite shell,
She's asking fish—"Did you hear it swell?"

Laughter dances in the breeze,
Tickling everyone with ease.
Jellyfish doing a jelly jig,
I join in, feeling quite big!

The Solace of Salt and Sky

A dog digs deep, finds a shoe,
He thinks it's treasure, isn't that true?
The waves agree, they crash and spin,
Is that a whale or just my kin?

Sunbathers wear hats like sails,
While crabs plot their goofy trails.
Seashells gossip about the tide,
Mermaids giggle, they can't hide!

Footsteps to an Enchanted Shore

Sandcastles lean, saying, "Oh please,
Don't let the tide bring us to our knees!"
A pelican jokes, "Catch me a fish!
But only if it's a grand little dish!"

Footprints dance to a whimsical beat,
Follow the laughter, it's oh so sweet.
A treasure map drawn in bright pink chalk,
Leading to where the sea cucumbers talk!

Songs of the Island's Children

Little feet on sandy shores,
Splashing water, chasing boars.
Coconut hats perched on heads,
Turning everyday into spreads.

Laughter echoes through the air,
Mango juice stains everywhere.
Crabs in chorus join the fun,
Underneath the blazing sun.

Pickles dance on wooden boats,
As fish jump and make their jokes.
Turtles play peek-a-boo with glee,
In a game of hide and seek, whee!

Joyful songs of youth resound,
Making mischief all around.
Island life is full of cheer,
With funny tales from far and near.

A Dance with Tropical Wildflowers

Tiny bugs with fancy moves,
Join the dance that nature proves.
Wildflowers sway in soft delight,
Winking at the stars at night.

Bananas wearing tutus bright,
Twirl around with pure delight.
Parrots whistling silly tunes,
While the sun smiles down like noons.

Swaying palms with breezy fans,
Making cool in flip-flop plans.
Mango trees in hula skirts,
Dropping fruit and quirkily flirts.

Nature's joy in every bloom,
Chasing butterflies with a zoom.
In the garden, fun's a game,
As every flower knows its name.

Visions of Sandy Footprints

Each tiny print tells a tale,
Of crabs dancing without fail.
The sun chases shadows away,
While waves sing a beachy sway.

Flip-flops fly in joyful play,
As children run in merry fray.
Sandcastles rise, then tumble down,
With giggles echoing all around.

Seashells whisper secrets sweet,
To eager ears, they dance to greet.
Footprints lead to treasure maps,
Of lost toys and giggling laps.

Every step, a memory spins,
As laughter mingles with the winds.
Sandy stories told with flair,
Make every day a sandy affair.

Celestial Dreams Beneath Starlit Skies

Underneath a blanket bright,
Dreamers dance in pure delight.
Fireflies twinkle, stealing beams,
While children weave their midnight dreams.

Stars are giggling in their glee,
Whispering secrets just for me.
Clouds take shape like silly things,
Maybe dragons with paper wings.

In the moonlight, shadows prance,
Taking part in the starry dance.
Tropical fruits join the fun,
As laughter sparkles, just like sun.

Celestial dreams drift and flow,
While sleepy heads with visions glow.
Every laugh, a star's embrace,
Filling the night with joy and grace.

Tropical Rainbows After the Storm

After rain, the sun does dance,
Colors pop in a wild prance.
I saw a fish wear a silly hat,
Singing loud, 'Hey, look at that!'

Pineapples rolling down the street,
Coconuts joining with their beat.
Every raindrop leaves a smile,
Who knew storms could be so worthwhile?

Hearts Anchored in Still Waters

A boat named 'Laughter' rocks with glee,
While waves tease crab and fish carefree.
Anchors drop to tickle fishy friends,
While every splash a giggle sends.

Seagulls joke as they snatch some fries,
While tanned folks just roll their eyes.
Fish flip-flop in a humorous show,
Dancing below in a buoyant flow.

The Language of the Sea Shells

Whispers of shells, they speak so loud,
Tales of mischief under the crowd.
A conch shell claimed a pirate's hat,
And laughed out front, 'Ain't I neat and fat?'

Tiny shells in a grand parade,
Waving hi, then a quick charade.
They gossip about the waves' strange ways,
Who knew shells could have such a phase?

Shadows of the Jungle's Lullaby

Monkeys sing a joyful tune,
Iguanas snooze beneath the moon.
A parrot squawks out a silly rhyme,
While all the critters keep perfect time.

Rustling leaves, a giggle or two,
A sloth waves and says, 'How do you do?'
In shadows deep, laughter unfolds,
With stories of jungle antics told.

The Adventure of Distant Horizons

On a boat with a chicken, we sailed the day,
The wind in our hair, making feathers play.
The captain yelled loudly, 'Don't eat my hat!'
While the waves laughed along, 'Oh, imagine that!'

We danced with the dolphins, our moves quite absurd,
They squealed in delight, not a single word.
A crab on a surfboard joined in the fun,
With sunglasses on, feeling quite like a pun.

Sailing past treasure, a pirate did frown,
He lost all his gold to a playful brown clown.
With a coconut drink, we toasted our luck,
While a parrot nearby yelled, 'What the... oh shucks!'

Just when we thought we'd found all the gold,
The map led us straight to a shriveled up mold.
But laughter is wealth, and we had it galore,
As we ventured to shores where adventure then soared.

Forgotten Songs of the Seven Seas

Sailors singing songs of socks gone astray,
As fish join the chorus in a glorious display.
The seaweed swayed gently like a hip-hop beat,
While starfish played tambourine with their feet.

A whale with a top hat took center stage,
Told jokes about krill that brought us all rage.
'Why don't they share?' was the punchline we heard,
And underwater laughter flapped like a bird.

Octopus played piano with whimsical grace,
While jellyfish boogied in a luminous space.
A sea turtle freestyled, quite out of his shell,
Said, 'If you're sea sick, just don't say it too well!'

As night fell, the stars twinkled bright like our dreams,
We gathered around for more musical schemes.
With treasures of laughter, we sung till the dawn,
The songs of the sea, a forever fun yawn.

Sails of Memory and Adventure

With sails that flopped like a tired cat,
We drifted past a dancing gnat.
Lost our way, but found some fries,
Who knew our boat could serve surprise?

The captain wore a hat so wide,
It caught the wind and caused a ride.
We soared in circles, spun around,
And laughed till our lost map was found.

Squawking birds joined our foolish tune,
While fish beneath us laughed at noon.
A mermaid waved from underneath,
'The best adventures start with a feast!'

So if you seek tales from the deep,
Keep your sense of humor - not sleep!
For every mishap starts the fun,
Just remember to pack a bun.

Twilight Reflections on Still Waters

As the sun dipped like a clumsy seal,
We dropped our snacks and made a meal.
Reflections danced like silly ghosts,
We clinked our cups and made some toasts.

The moon crept in like a quiet thief,
Stealing our snacks gave us grief.
We paddled our boat, a floating mess,
With ripples echoing our silliness.

A frog in a tie played the fiddle,
While we attempted some silly riddle.
The fish pooled around in sheer delight,
Watching us bumble into the night.

So when the dusk whispers our names,
And lanterns flicker with playful flames,
We'll dance on shores, with laughter to share,
Collecting the joys that float in the air.

Beneath the Banyan's Embrace

Beneath the branches, a curious spot,
A hammock swung that got too hot.
We tried to nap, but the bugs had plans,
They formed a band and danced on hands.

The tree whispered secrets in soft, silly tones,
While a squirrel critiqued our funky moans.
We joined the concert, a versus choir,
Who knew our laughter could inspire?

An iguana too joined the glee,
Rolling his eyes at a laughing bee.
We picnicked on sandwiches – half a slice,
Who knew ants could be so precise?

So here's to moments, a tangled embrace,
With friends around and a merry space.
To laugh, to wiggle, make life our play,
Just beneath the banyan, we frolic away.

The Rhythm of Lapping Waves

The waves came in, a bubbly crew,
They lapped at our toes, with a playful coo.
We leaped and splashed, a fishy dance,
Till one lost their shoe in a daring prance.

A crab in a shell had humor to spare,
He challenged our balance with a cunning stare.
We tripped on sand, fell with a crash,
The waves chuckled back with a merry splash.

Seagulls squawked, they knew the tune,
While we tried to sing like a goofy loon.
The rhythm of laughter, the waves kept time,
Who knew chaos could feel so sublime?

We'll dance with the tide, till the sun goes low,
For in every ripple, a funny tale flows.
So when life's a splash, just belly flop,
The ocean's our stage, let the laughter never stop.

Shadows Dancing on the Marina

In the boat, a seagull squawks,
While fishermen tease with silly talks.
The sun dips down, with a wink so sly,
I swear that dolphin just rolled by!

The dock's a stage for clumsy moves,
As tourists stumble, trying to groove.
A crab scuttles, giving me the eye,
I laugh as it seems to dance nearby!

With ice cream drips on sandy toes,
In this warm breeze, everyone knows.
The laughter echoes, no reason to care,
As shadows jive in the salty air!

So come on down, let worries flee,
Join the show, oh can't you see?
The marina's life, a goofy spree,
Where smiles abound, wild and free!

The Call of the Distant Islands

In the distance, a parrot squawks,
It's time for tales and silly talks.
The horizon hums a jaunty tune,
As sunburned tourists dance beneath the moon!

A crab on a kayak, what a sight!
Paddling fast, oh what a fright!
The locals giggle at the bold display,
While tourists try to imitate their sway!

Jokes are tossed like seashells thrown,
In this paradise, we're never alone.
Sipping coconut drinks, we take our time,
Life's a beach—come join the rhyme!

So heed the call, leave worries behind,
Embrace the mischief that's intertwined.
As laughter echoes across the sand,
We find our fun in this sun-kissed land!

Rippling Reflections on Calm Seas

Waves gently chuckle, a playful tease,
While jellyfish jiggle with motley ease.
A slapstick splash from a careless dive,
It's a comedy show, and we're alive!

The sun does wink, a golden sheen,
As paddleboards glide, looking serene.
A clumsy fall leads to laughter loud,
Even the fish seem impressed and proud!

With each ripple, tales start to flow,
Of pirates and mermaids, and seashells aglow.
In this calm, giggles float like the tide,
Where fun and joy are our greatest guide!

So cast your worries into the deep,
Dance with the waves, let the ocean sweep.
With every splash, there's magic to find,
A funny life, playful and kind!

Moments Caught Between the Tides

Between the tides, a crab plays tag,
Chasing the sun, it runs without lag.
With every wave, a new story starts,
As children giggle and share their hearts!

A flip-flop flies, caught in the breeze,
It lands on a fish, oh what a tease!
The crowd erupts with a hearty cheer,
As laughter warms this seaside sphere!

Sandcastles rise, with shells as crowns,
While seagulls swoop, scaring the frowns.
The waves perform a comedic dance,
We laugh together, take a chance!

So gather close as the sun dips low,
In these moments, let your joy overflow.
Between the tides, where dreams collide,
We find pure fun, with hearts open wide!

Serenity Painted in Aquamarine

The waves giggle as they crash,
Sunbathers flip and fall with class.
Seagulls squawk in a raucous choir,
While sandcastle kings aspire.

Umbrellas dance, lost in the breeze,
Old men nap, dreaming of cheese.
Children chase their dreams in foam,
Only to find the tide's their home.

The sun waves goodbye, just for fun,
As daffy dolphins leap and run.
With giggles bright, a joyful scene,
Life's a beach painted in aquamarine.

An octopus waves, all eight in sync,
Wearing a hat, oh what do you think?
A party's brewing in the kelp,
Come join the fun! Just don't eat your phelps.

Coconuts and Quiet Reflections

A coconut fell, bonked on my head,
I thought it was a message from the dead.
Sipping the milk, I ponder deep,
What if it rains, and no one will sleep?

The crabs are plotting, I swear it's true,
Wearing tiny hats and sneaky shoes.
While fish join in for the conga line,
I take a sip, this coconut's mine!

The sunset chuckles, painting the skies,
As pelicans swirl and steal the fries.
Reflections ripple, laughter so loud,
We're all here, feeling quite proud.

So cheers to the fruits that fall from the trees,
Bringing joy with every breeze.
With coconuts here to lighten the mood,
I laugh, I sip, my day's been renewed.

Daydreams Adrift on Gentle Currents

There's a turtle wearing sunglasses bright,
Floating by, what a silly sight!
Fish are giggling, tickled by glee,
As daydreams drift on the soft, warm sea.

A crab's telling jokes, oh what a treat,
With a punchline that can't be beat!
Seaweed sways and dances around,
While the sun plays hide and seek with sound.

Mermaids splashing, singing in tune,
Under the gaze of the sleepy moon.
Their laughter bubbles, a joyful cheer,
In this paradise, all worries disappear.

With jellyfish blushing, floating so light,
They join the party, oh what a sight!
So let's drift on currents, carefree and wise,
In this wacky world, joy never dies.

The Legend of the Lighthouse Keeper

Once a keeper with a lighthouse beam,
Cooked fish stew and made quite the scene.
With a parrot squawking tales of old,
His lighthouse stood strong, never cold.

Visitors came, all lost at sea,
For the keeper's lighthouse was the key.
He'd wave to ships with a big, goofy grin,
While his cat plotted how to sneak in.

One stormy night, the light went out,
The keeper cursed, let out a shout.
But with a flick, he solved the plight,
And sent the ships back to the right night.

Now legends say if you listen close,
You'll hear the laughter of the friendly ghost.
The keeper's joy, like a starry keeper's glow,
Guides all lost sailors to safely row.

Kaleidoscope of Sunset Colors

As the sun dips low, a grand display,
Colors swirl and twist, in a playful ballet.
Even the seagulls wear shades of pink,
While crabs on the shore share a wink and a blink.

The ocean giggles, waves dance up high,
Clouds in silly hats float lazily by.
A turtle in a top hat, what a sight!
Recites a sea shanty, keeping things light.

Fishes in bow ties swim in a rush,
Joining the clam band for a coral hush.
Underwater parties where everyone's cool,
Even the starfish know how to rule.

So let's toast to sunsets that brighten our day,
With laughter and joy, come on, let's play!
For in this vivid show of colors divine,
Life on the shores is simply fine!

Elysium of Forgotten Shores

Where the sand seems to giggle beneath our toes,
The laughter of waves as everyone knows.
Seashells tell secrets with each ebb and flow,
While the driftwood beards start to mimic the show.

Crabs in their dance, they sneak and they scurry,
Waving their claws, oh so proud in a flurry.
The sun lost its hat, and the beach gets a laugh,
As a dolphin breaks free and poses for a photograph.

Forgotten shores filled with treasures untold,
Where pineapples tumble like stories of old.
The ice cream truck sails 'neath a sky full of blobs,
Laughter erupts over goofy beach mobs.

Each wave a tickle, a gentle embrace,
In silly old Elysium, it's all about grace.
Every giggle echoed by the wind's sweet refrain,
Reminding us here, to be young once again!

Tides of Serenity

As the tides roll in, the sand starts to play,
With a flip-flop tango, leading us astray.
Sandcastles giggle, top hats made of seaweed,
Crabs on parade, living their childhood creed.

A beach ball's a friend, bouncing high in the air,
While gulls crack a joke, without a care.
With each gentle wave, the beach rocks along,
Tide pools are singing their own silly song.

Frolicking fishes in a splashy charade,
Making funny faces in a salty cascade.
Seashells collect laughs, each one a delight,
As the moon starts to glow, a whimsical light.

So come kick off your shoes, join the whimsy we find,
Where each wave brings laughter and peace intertwined.
Tides of serenity, fun lives through the night,
With every new wave, the world feels just right!

Whispering Palms

In the sway of the palms, secrets unfold,
Each rustling leaf with a story to be told.
Palms gossip like teenagers, giggles on breeze,
Bending so low, they just want to tease.

A parrot retorts with a colorful squawk,
Joined by the geckos in a silly walk.
With sunglasses in place, they chuckle away,
In the shade of the palms, mischief holds sway.

Dancing coconuts swing to an unheard beat,
While the sun sets in stripes, a colorful seat.
Tiki torches flicker, casting shadows with flair,
As crickets conduct a night-time affair.

So lift up your spirits, let laughter prevail,
In a land of absurd, where joy sets the sail.
Whispering palms share the joy with delight,
In this comical corner, everything feels light!

Coconuts and Coral Dreams

Coconuts fall with a thud,
As we dance on the warm, wet sand.
Crabs join the fun, quite a stud,
Pinching toes with their little hand.

A parrot squawks a silly tune,
As fish swim by in a fishy dance.
Under the sun, we sing in June,
While dolphins giggle at our prance.

Tropical drinks with umbrellas bright,
We sip while lounging in our seats.
The sunset's glow, oh what a sight,
Even the stars join in with beats!

On this shore, laughter is king,
Every wave brings a cheerful cheer.
A joyous breeze is all we bring,
In this paradise, all's good here!

A Canvas of Cerulean Horizons

Painted skies, oh what a view,
As we splash in the turquoise sea.
With brushes made of laughter too,
Monkeys giggle at you and me.

The sun's a circus, high and round,
Juggling clouds like a playful mime.
Seagulls squawk, they're quite profound,
Stealing fries, oh what a crime!

We try to swim, but cats just float,
With jellyfish doing the cha-cha.
The sandcastles shout, 'Hey, we wrote,
Your beach vacation's a drama!'

As night falls down like a blanket,
Frogs sing songs of sweet serenades.
We laugh, we rhyme, we lightly prank it,
In dreams of colors, joy cascades!

The Spirit of Lullabies and Lighthouses

Lighthouses wink like cheeky pets,
Guiding boats beyond the reef.
A gentle breeze, no regrets,
As we giggle with disbelief.

Sailboats race on a silly spree,
While sea turtles laugh in disguise.
The rhythm of waves is a melody,
That tickles our ears and our eyes.

Time to claim our coconut prize,
Swinging from palms with honks and chirps.
Under the moon, we warn the spies,
From hungry sharks with their playful jerks!

With lullabies sung to the stars,
We dance like fireflies in the air.
Each twinkle reminds us of ours,
In this haven, we've not a care!

Mysteries of the Lagoon's Depth

Under the surface, a giggle awaits,
Fish throw a party, it's all the rage.
With seaweed confetti and silly plates,
It's an underwater, laughing stage!

A crab does the limbo; a turtle winks,
While an octopus juggles its snacks.
Guppies swim by, giving us blinks,
While eels poke their heads through cracks.

The secrets they keep, so wild and free,
Bubble up like laughter, we can't resist.
What wonders lie down, come take a spree,
Kissing the shadows—who could've guessed?

The lagoon's a treasure, full of delight,
Where stories are spun in a playful jest.
Each ripple of water, a dance in the night,
Our hearts stay light, this is simply the best!

Windswept Love Letters

A breeze blew letters, they danced and twirled,
Penning sweet notes in a salty-fish world.
Seagulls squawked gossip, the wind took its shot,
'This message needs jelly, or maybe it's not!'

With hearts full of laughter, they sailed through the skies,
Each word a cheeky wink, oh how love defies!
I'll send you my heart in a bottle, no less,
But it's caught in the coral, such a messy distress!

Amidst all the giggles, a message went wrong,
It read, 'You're my marlin!' instead of 'My song!'
Together they chuckled, a twist of the fate,
For love's just a pun in a fishy old state!

So here's to the letters that flutter and flow,
With winds of affection, and laughter aglow.
In a sea full of whimsy, our spirits will dance,
Forever entangled in joy and in chance.

Legends Carved in Driftwood

Driftwood tales whispered upon the warm sand,
Of mermaids who knit with a clam for a hand.
A crab wrote a story, it got lost on a beach,
Where the waves laughed so hard, their laughter would screech!

The tales of old sailors are tied to the tide,
One claimed to have danced with a dolphin, a bride!
But legend has it, while they tangoed with flair,
The dolphin just rolled, said, 'Get off, you're bare!'

A lighthouse out in the blue had a light that was dim,
It moaned and it groaned, 'My bulbs are too slim!'
They brought it a ladder, a crank and a bulb,
But the light just sighed out loud, 'I need a club!'

So here on the shores where the legends all roam,
People gather 'round driftwood to craft them a home.
With laughter like waves that crash and recede,
The treasures of humor are all that we need.

A Tapestry of Sea and Sky

Under skies that tease, where the fish wear a grin,
The clouds are the artists, with dolphins to spin.
They inked sunny doodles on the canvas so bright,
While octopuses knitted the stars into night!

A turtle named Timmy, with dreams to explore,
Took a selfie with seagulls, called it 'creature galore!'
He said with a wink, 'I'm a star down below,'
But he tripped on a wave and got splashed with a 'no!'

The colors of laughter, they swirl in our hearts,
Like fish in a frenzy, each tickle imparts.
We're woven together in giggles and grace,
With a tapestry shimmering, a whimsical place!

So let's sail with the winds, let our spirits run free,
In a world painted funny, as vast as the sea.
With the sun in our sails and the moon as our guide,
We'll laugh through the waves, with joy by our side.

Solace Among the Lavender Seas

In lavender waves where the giggles run deep,
Fish wear polka-dots, they wiggle and leap.
A whale with a hat sings a tune quite absurd,
'This sea's all about fun,' it proudly declared!

The stars are like sprinkles, all golden and bright,
Pouring down giggles that dance through the night.
A crab joins the chorus with tap dance delight,
While jellyfish sway to the rhythm of light!

With snickers and chuckles, the sea tells its tale,
Of mermaids with bubblegum, sailing a whale.
Their laughter echoes through the waters so wide,
'Cause joy's in the ocean, let's take it for a ride!

So throw out your anchors on shores made of smile,
In lavender seas where we pause for a while.
With comrades who giggle, and skies filled with cheer,
We'll savor this solace, let laughter steer!

Whispers of Tropical Breezes

A coconut fell with a thud,
The parrot squawked, 'What a dud!'
The beach ball bounced on the sand,
Sunburned tourists looking bland.

Wind's a tease, it steals my hat,
The crab just blinked; what's up with that?
Tanned folks juggling fruit with flair,
While seagulls plan their next affair.

Children splash, and laughter flies,
A sunscreen war beneath the skies.
Flip-flops lost in a guessing game,
Polka dots and stripes, never the same!

Sipping cocktails with little umbrellas,
Watching antics of sneaky fella.
Life's a joke, the tide will sway,
In this paradise, we laugh and play.

Secrets Beneath the Canopy

Under leaves where shadows creep,
Monkeys chatter, never sleep.
Sneaky snakes on leafy trails,
Imagine tales of epic fails!

A frog jumps high, but what a flop,
Next to him, a log should hop!
Whispers swirl within the trees,
Tell me, do those toucans tease?

A squirrel drops his nutly prize,
It lands right on my friend's surprise.
Laughter echoes, the parrots screech,
Nature's humor? It's quite the teach!

A raccoon strolls, looks quite suave,
Stealing berries, oh look at him thrive!
In this place of wondrous sounds,
Life's a joke that knows no bounds.

Echoes of the Ocean Tides

Waves crash down, a dramatic scene,
Flip-flops lost, my foot's the queen!
Seashells giggle, the crabs are shy,
"Don't take my home!" I hear them cry.

The surfboard's missing, where did it go?
A dolphin laughs at my woe,
Beachcombers search for treasures rare,
Only to find a flip-flop pair!

The tide retreats with a playful grin,
Waves whisper secrets; let the fun begin!
Sandy sandwiches, a picnic to share,
Seagulls dive down, claiming their fare.

Shells tell tales of what's been tossed,
In salty wonder, we'll not be lost.
In every splash, a giggle awaits,
As laughter dances with ocean's fates.

Dances of the Palm Fronds

Palm fronds sway to a rhythm unique,
A lizard twirls; it's quite the freak!
Pirate hats and grass skirts too,
Who knew that palms could shake like you?

A hula troupe made of coconuts,
Beneath their sway, even grass cuts!
Dancing shadows, the sun's a DJ,
Let's hula hoop and twist away.

The monkeys clap with great delight,
While tourists whirl in the warm sunlight.
Palm leaves rustle; they groove along,
Watch out, there's a coconut with a song!

As dusk falls, the vibe stays bright,
Stars join in; oh, what a sight!
The fronds keep dancing, joy on the air,
In this silly soirée, we haven't a care.

Blooming Amongst the Seafoam

Tiny crabs dance on the sand,
With shells that glow, oh, isn't it grand?
A fish with a hat swims by with flair,
While seagulls squawk like they just don't care.

Coconuts giggle in the palm tree's sway,
As monkeys swing and shout, "Let's play!"
The sun wears shades, sipping coconut milk,
While beach towels flutter like a patchwork quilt.

Starfish gossip as they rest on the floor,
"Oh, do you hear? The waves want more!"
They plan a parade with shells as their crowns,
While flip-flops dance and the laughter drowns.

The tide rolls in with a mischievous grin,
"Who's up for a splash? Let the fun begin!"
Amidst the seafoam, joy takes its place,
With nature's own smile, life's a big race.

Tales from the Island Breeze

The breeze tells tales that tickle the palm,
Of fishes in tuxedos who swim so calm.
A pelican sings with a voice so deep,
While crabs share secrets of treasures they keep.

In flip-flops, the locals sway to the beat,
While beach balls bounce with no hint of defeat.
The sun on their backs, they twirl and they spin,
"Who needs shoes? Let the fun just begin!"

A dolphin jumps in a whirl of delight,
Chasing after a kite that took off in flight.
The sandcastle kings and queens take their stand,
While seashells cheer from the enchanted land.

Every gust giggles and whispers a tune,
Telling of mischief under the moon.
A celebration of life in each dancing wave,
In this island oasis, the bold and the brave.

Guardians of the Shoreline

Turtles in sunglasses patrol the sand,
With shells painted bright, they form a cool band.
A crab turns DJ, spinning seashells to beat,
While starfish twirl, showing off fancy feet.

A pelican referee plays with a whistle,
"Foul play!" he squawks, as the waves start to bristle.
The seagulls complain, "Not enough room!"
As the dolphins dive, making all the waves bloom.

Lighthouses giggle, standing tall and bright,
Guiding the ships with their own kind of light.
"Watch out for splashes!" the sea-foam warns,
As laughter erupts with the rise of the morn.

The shoreline stands as a lively parade,
With characters dressed in the sun and the shade.
Every grain of sand knows the giggling lore,
Of comrades and capers on this ocean floor.

Mangrove Shadows at Dusk

In the mangrove shadows, where laughter is play,
The crickets sing of adventures each day.
A frog with a crown croaks stories so grand,
While fireflies twinkle, making magic unplanned.

The monkeys swing low, with pranks on their mind,
While iguanas nod, a wise watchful kind.
They snicker and chatter, plotting their schemes,
As the sunset hugs the water in dreams.

Every rustle of leaves holds a secret or two,
"Who stole my banana? Oh, it must be you!"
The tide whispers gossip, soft like a sigh,
As laughter entwines with the evening sky.

The moon peeks down, shining soft on the land,
And the shadows dance, a joyful band.
In the quiet of dusk, with funny surprise,
Nature's own humor is the greatest prize.

Nightfall's Cuddle by the Sea

As the sun takes a dive, the moon slips by,
Seagulls giggle, waves whisper, oh my!
A crab in a tux, just scuttled on stage,
While starfish dance, it's all the rage.

The sand's a blanket, so cozy and warm,
Where jellybeans bounce, causing such charm.
A dolphin does flips, with a wink and a grin,
Who knew the ocean could have such spin!

Shells hum a tune, the coconuts sway,
Palm trees are swaying, let's dance and play!
The air is a fizz, like soda in flight,
As night wraps around us—what a delight!

So let's toast to the stars, raise our cups high,
With laughter and joy, it's a silly sky.
Turtles join in, wearing party hats tight,
Under nightfall's cuddle, everything's right.

Fishing for Stars in Twilight Waters

With rods made of giggles, we cast out our dreams,
In waters so splashy, with sparkly beams.
A mermaid named Lucy, she grins with a wink,
Her fishy friends swim, in colors that blink.

We bait with our laughter, and hope for a bite,
As octopuses juggle, what a funny sight!
The stars start to twinkle, like fireflies free,
In this zany world, it's a riotous spree.

The tides tell us tales, of seaweed so bold,
Where crumpets have tea, and the sea cows are gold.
A big finned fish shows us his latest dance,
And we join in, hoping to take a chance.

With a splash and a laugh, our evening unfolds,
In twilight's soft glow, our joy ever holds.
As we fish for the stars, with each silly quirk,
The night spins around, with no hint of work.

Stories Written in Golden Sand

Every grain holds a giggle, a story to tell,
Of pirates who tripped, and a clam with a shell.
A treasure map scribbled, in jelly and goo,
Leads to underwater, where the laughs just grew.

An octopus scribe writes in bubbles with glee,
Of hearts made of sea foam, so wild and free.
Each wave brings a whisper, tickling our toes,
As we chase the stories, where silliness flows.

Footprints in the sand—a dance on the shore,
As crabs clap their claws, for a silly encore.
With shells made for hats, and seaweed for ties,
The wind plays a tune, under giggling skies.

So gather your stories, spin tales of delight,
For in every grain, there's a spark shining bright.
We'll build castles of laughter, till the tides softly land,
Where memories linger, written in golden sand.

A Paradise of Lost Dreams

In a land where the flip-flops dance through the air,
Dreams lie on the beach, without a single care.
A treasure chest filled with mismatched old socks,
Plays hide and seek with the curious rocks.

The sea nymphs giggle, their hair full of foam,
In this paradise, there's no need for a home.
With wishes tied up in a bubblegum bow,
We chase after rainbows, and let our minds flow.

Sandcastles topple, oh what a grand mess,
As the crabs throw a party, don't you dare stress!
With shells as our pillows and grasshoppers' song,
We'll dance through the night, where the silly belongs.

So let's laugh at our fumbles, embrace the wild night,
For in this lost paradise, everything's right.
With dreams in our pockets, let happiness gleam,
As we skip down the shore, it's a glorious dream.

Secrets Beneath the Waves

The fish wear suits, oh what a sight,
They hold their meetings deep at night.
Clams gossip loudly, pearls in their eyes,
Scuba divers wondering, 'Are they wise?'

Octopuses dance in their own parade,
They flip through the seaweed, quite unafraid.
Crabs take selfies, posing quite proud,
While seahorses chuckle, forming a crowd.

Starfish compete for the best tan,
While squids make faces, as only they can.
Sudden laughs echo from a hidden reef,
As turtles roll over, feeling quite chief.

So if you dive beneath the sea blue,
Remember the laughter, it's all just for you.
Secrets and giggles swirl in the tide,
You might just find friends, if you look wide.

Echoes of the Tropical Storm

Raindrops tap-dance on rooftops with glee,
While trees try to hold on, precariously.
Puddles become ponds, with frogs all around,
Jumping and croaking, a wild, joyful sound.

Coconuts tumble, it's quite a scene,
As parrots complain, feeling quite mean.
Lizards slide by, in a hurry to flee,
While flowers are laughing, 'Oh, let it be!'

Waves crash and giggle upon the shore,
While crabs in their burrows just hunker and snore.
The wind tells secrets with a mischievous grin,
As palm trees sway, letting the fun begin.

So, next time it storms, don't you despair,
Join in the chaos, if you dare!
Nature's a jester, so let it perform,
And dance in delight through the tropical storm.

The Dance of Coral Shadows

Coral reefs sway, in a buoyant ballet,
As fish leap and twirl, in a colorful display.
Anemones wiggle, inviting a hug,
While clownfish chuckle, feeling quite smug.

Jellyfish drift like balloons in the blue,
Making faces at turtles, who laugh back too.
Angelfish prance, in their glitzy attire,
While shrimp steal the spotlight, never to tire.

Mantis shrimp boast, with their flashy new moves,
While sea urchins scowl, watching the grooves.
Crustaceans tap dance, on the reef's sandy floor,
Creating a ruckus; oh, what's in store?

With laughter and colors, the ocean's a show,
Join in the fun, let your wild side grow.
Dive deep for the magic, it's waiting for you,
In the dance of shadows, where laughter is true.

Sunrise Over Silent Shores

The sun peeks in, with a yawn and a stretch,
While seagulls are circling, all keen to fetch.
Sandcastles shimmer, wearing golden crowns,
As crabs patrol, wearing tiny frowns.

Waves giggle softly, brushing the land,
Shells wake from slumber, all perfectly planned.
A dog runs by, with joy in its bark,
While beachcomber trips on a wayward shark.

The sky throws a party, in orange and pink,
As dolphins debate, "What do you think?"
The tide rolls in, with secrets to tell,
And laughter erupts, like a magical spell.

So greet the new day, with a chuckle or two,
Embrace all the wonders, the joy born anew.
On silent shores, let the fun begin,
For life in the sun is the best kind of win.

Beneath the Coconut Canopy

Coconuts drop like thunderclaps,
As I dodge and weave like a pro,
The locals laugh, they know my snares,
But I just grin, putting on a show.

Monkeys swing and chatter loud,
Snatching snacks from unsuspecting hands,
While I try to fit in with the crowd,
Mimicking moves, making strange plans.

A parrot squawks a joke or two,
I respond, but no one can tell,
Is it my dance or my bad drawl?
Either way, I'm under its spell.

Palm trees sway in laughter's tune,
As the sun dips low with a wink,
With each slip and trip, I'm a cartoon,
Making memories faster than a blink.

Melodies of the Ocean Breeze

Waves crash, a symphony galore,
But I play a tune with a broken shell,
Seagulls join with their off-key score,
Still, I hum along; it's fine, oh well!

Footprints in sand, an island dance,
Splashing water, laughing with glee,
I trip on a crab, it's got no chance,
Together we tumble — the best of me!

The tide rolls in, pulling me near,
To find treasures buried, oh what a thrill!
But instead, I just see my lost flip-flop here,
I joke with the shore, it's just my luck still.

Underneath the sun, we let loose,
Chasing giggles with every wave,
I'll serenade crabs, and they'll let me choose,
The ocean's laughter makes me brave.

Island Dreams in Starlit Skies

Twinkling lights like disco balls,
The moon winks down, it's quite a sight,
I'm dancing with shadows, heedless of falls,
Laughing with stars, feeling just right.

In the hammock, I sway to the breeze,
A snooze turns to snoring, I hear the jokes,
The stars are my friends; they giggle with ease,
As the night unfolds, it's where laughter pokes.

Crickets chirp in a rhythmic beat,
While I dream of tacos and silly hats,
I'm the king of mischief, not missing a beat,
With dreams concocted beneath chatting chats.

The stars start to yawn, it's closing time,
Yet I dance with my dreams, what a scene,
Stopping the night with a verse and a rhyme,
Tomorrow I'll rule, or so it might seem.

Solitude Wrapped in a Sea Breeze

Sitting alone with my coconut drink,
The ocean whispers tales, none too clear,
I ponder life while trying not to blink,
As seagulls squawk, I tip my beer!

A crab rolls by, I'd join him in dance,
But he sidesteps—oh how rude it seems,
With every sway, I give it a chance,
To bust some moves in my island dreams.

The breeze plays tricks with my hair so wild,
Each strand's a rebel, a playful tease,
Like a child throwing tantrums, so unbeguiled,
I smile wide while surrendering to ease.

Laughing with solitude, a duo divine,
As fish race past in a watery spree,
In this funny tale, I'm feeling just fine,
Wrapped in breezes, I'm totally free.

Beneath a Veil of Tropical Rain

Raindrops play a silly tune,
While I dance like a cartoon.
Coconuts drop, and so do I,
Splashing puddles, oh my, oh my!

A parrot squawks with glee and cheer,
"Dance around, it's wet out here!"
I slip and slide, a clumsy show,
But in this chaos, joy will grow!

The palm trees sway, they start to laugh,
As I take a thrilling bath.
A swim in flip-flops, watch me glide,
In this silly storm, I'll take pride!

With giggles loud, I find my way,
In puddles deep, oh what a play!
The rain keeps falling, let it pour,
I'll splash forever, who could ask for more?

Waves of Memory on a Summer Day

Waves crash in a wobbly dance,
As I try to catch a glance.
A seagull swoops, I duck to hide,
And my sandwich goes for a ride!

The sun shines down, a fiery ball,
As sunscreen turns me white as wall.
I lather up and slip around,
Like a fish, I flop, yet find no ground!

A flip-flop flies, it's on a spree,
With my laughter as company.
The beach is full of silly sights,
As we chase crabs, oh what delights!

With buckets high and castles grand,
We build a throne on sun-kissed sand.
But with a wave, it crumbles down,
Now I'm just the kid with a frown!

Shelter Among the Banyan Roots

Beneath the branches, twisted wide,
I found a nook to laugh and hide.
The roots tickle as I recline,
This jungle gym is truly fine!

A monkey swings, he makes me grin,
He steals my hat and runs to win.
I chase him round the ancient trees,
He hands it back, with much unease!

The humidity gives me a sweat,
But in this shade, I have no regret.
With friends around, we share a joke,
We scare the bugs, and chainsaw smoke!

Wooden swings made from vines and ropes,
We launch ourselves, igniting hopes.
Laughter rings through leafy lanes,
As nature plays its funny games!

Sunrise Serenade Among the Cliffs

Morning breaks with laughter bright,
As I chase the sun, a fiery sight.
The gulls are singing their soft tune,
While I stumble—oops!—I greet the moon!

On rocky ledges, I take a stand,
With coffee splashed across my hand.
The waves call out with playful roars,
As I ponder life and its wild shores!

A crab scuttles, quick as a thought,
I try to catch him; I'm just distraught!
He gives me a look—oh! What a stare,
Saying, "What's this? A hairless bear?"

Sunrise blooms with colors bold,
While I sip, feeling oh-so-gold.
With giggles shared and joy in air,
This cliffside life, I've no compare!

Island Time in a Bottle

Sipping rum under the palm's sway,
Seagulls squawk, chase my cares away.
Time's a trickster on sandy shores,
Who needs clocks? Just open more doors!

Flip-flops squeak in the warm sun glow,
Lost my hat, but gained a new bro.
The tide does a dance, a splash and a slide,
While I try balancing a coconut ride!

Coconuts whisper secrets to trees,
While crabs pinch toes like curious thieves.
I laugh so hard, I snort with glee,
Island time's a treasure, wild and free!

With every sunset, the skies ignite,
I wonder if the stars could dance all night.
So here's to joy, on this playful spree,
In a bottle of sunshine, come sip with me!

The Last Dolphin's Song

A dolphin hums the silliest tune,
As beach balls bounce in the afternoon.
With a flip and a wiggle, he makes a show,
Who knew fish could have such a flow?

"Join me!" he chirps, with a splashy delight,
While I try swimming—what a silly sight!
He twirls around, giving me the fins,
Together we giggle, sharing oceanic wins.

Mackerels laugh, they're belly-aching,
Wondering why my own legs are shaking.
But the last song is one of pure fun,
As we drift on waves, under the sun.

The beach is a stage, seaweed our props,
With laughter that echoes and never stops.
So let's sail with the breeze, keep chasing that light,
And sing with the dolphins till stars say goodnight!

Deserted Beaches and Heartbeats

On a beach where no one else roams,
Shells whisper secrets; they sing like poems.
I chased a sand crab, but he got away,
Now I'm left with my thoughts and sun's glorious ray.

Waves tickle toes that wiggle in sand,
A coconut hat, my own fashion brand!
With a splash and a laugh, I slip and I slide,
The only audience is the tide and my pride.

Starfish gather for a quirky dance,
While I join in, giving clams a chance.
Oh, deserted beaches, how alive you feel,
With heartbeats echoing, meters of zeal!

In this world, no one judges my way,
Just me and my silliness, come what may.
With giggles and splashes, I'll stay here awhile,
On deserted shores where laughter's the style!

Coral Gardens Under Moonlit Skies

Beneath the moon, the corals giggle,
As fish in bow ties dance and wiggle.
A sea turtle joins the late-night ball,
With jellyfish lights that dazzle and enthrall!

"Who's got the best moves?" the clownfish boast,
While I just float, trying to coast.
The octopus spins with eight arms out wide,
I can't help but chuckle, it's quite a ride!

The sea anemones wave with delight,
As we twirl around in shimmering light.
Can't remember my moves, but who even cares?
In coral gardens, no one has snares.

So let's dive deeper, unravel the night,
With laughter and joy, everything feels right.
Under moonlit skies, we'll dance till we drop,
In these gardens of laughter, we'll never stop!

The Rhythm of Island Life

Laughter echoes on the shore,
A crab dances, asking for more.
With palm trees swaying in tune,
The sun smiles bright, a cheeky afternoon.

Tropical drinks with umbrellas bright,
Monkeys join in, what a sight!
Turtles snack on seaweed pie,
Island style, oh me, oh my!

Fishing boats bobbing like kids at play,
They all swear they'll catch fish today.
But the only thing that bites is the bait,
And the seagulls plot to celebrate!

Cool breezes whisper through the night,
While fireflies dance, oh what a flight!
The rhythm rolls like waves that sway,
"Oh my gosh!" someone laughs, "Not again, Jay!"

Hidden Bays and Lush Greens

Behind the trees, a cove appears,
Where the local fish laugh at fears.
With coconuts falling, plop, plop, plop,
And beachcombers shouting, "Oh, look what I've got!"

A hammock swings with humorous grace,
As someone leaps, but misses the space.
They land in the sand, a soft, cushy flop,
While turtles snicker and never stop!

Lush greens hide secrets and dreams,
Flowers giggle, or so it seems.
Underneath the canopy, shadows play,
"Did you bring snacks?" a parrot would say!

Hidden trails twist, a merry maze,
Each step brings new laughs and praise.
Nature's jester, vibrant and keen,
Painting smiles in every scene.

Footprints in the White Sand

Tiny toes tread soft and light,
Leaving footprints, a comical sight.
"Look at my path!" a child beams wide,
As seagulls laugh, oh what a stride!

Bouncing crabs scuttle and scorn,
As they dodge the shadow of a norm.
In the race of who goes faster,
I swear, that crab's a true master!

Footprints lead to treasure or snack,
With snacks in bags we forgot to pack.
"Did someone steal my sandwich again?"
The laughter rolls like ocean's zen.

By the tide, footprints wash joyfully,
Leaving giggles in the frothy spree.
"Oh look," cries a kid, "There's my shoe!"
It's a fish now, what's a kid to do?

Hibiscus Blooming Underneath the Sun

Under bright skies, petals dance,
Hibiscus prancing in summer's romance.
"Can you smell that?" a friend insists,
While bees buzz off, they can't resist.

A picnic set, colors collide,
As ants form a party, plans to slide.
"Watch my sandwich! Oh no! 'Tis gone!"
The hibiscus giggles, it's on the lawn!

The sun shines bright, a playful tease,
Filling beachgoers with bliss and ease.
"Who wore sunscreen?" someone yells,
While laughter trails like dreamy bells.

At sunset, colors blend and swirl,
Kids chase shadows in a twirly whirl.
"Look at me!", they shout with glee,
As the flowers wink, "Join us, carefree!"

Winged Wonders in the Tropic Breeze

Parrots squawk with silly flair,
Dancing feathers in warm air.
A pelican takes a clumsy dive,
Lands in fish—what a way to thrive!

Seagulls steal a sandwich, bold,
While beachgoers watch, uncontrolled.
Each bird a comedian in disguise,
Cracking jokes beneath sunny skies.

Coconuts roll with a playful dash,
While crabs scuttle in a frantic flash.
Laughter erupts as they race along,
In this realm where mischief belongs.

Under palm shade, the fun montages,
Everyone laughs at nature's mirages.
With winged wonders playing around,
Joy is found where the sea meets ground.

Memories Cradled by the Sea

A crab in a hat takes center stage,
Slow-motion shuffle, the crowd engages.
Seashells whisper tales so dear,
Of laughter shared, it's crystal clear.

Kids chase waves with galloping feet,
While mom's sunbathing, trying to cheat.
Seagulls squawk, they know the bet,
Stealing fries—what a clever set!

Every splash and every cheer,
Makes time freeze, a frozen sphere.
Sandcastles crumble, a sandstorm's plea,
Moments stored by the restless sea.

Bottled laughter sways with the tide,
Memories crafted where joy can't hide.
In this playground of glimmer and glee,
Life's absurd in a dance with the sea.

Whispering Winds of Abandon

Breezes giggle as they sneak,
Through palm fronds, a game they seek.
Laughter rustles through the trees,
While squirrels plot their nutty fees.

A hammock sways, a pirate's dream,
While flowers scheme a sneaky beam.
A leaf falls, a surprise in flight,
A leaf that lands on the dog—what a sight!

Chasing shadows, cheeky and bold,
Winds tickle toes in the afternoon gold.
The day laughs back, a glorious tease,
As breeze and creatures conspire to please.

In this land of whim and play,
Where every gust brings a new foray.
The whispers swirl, they won't relent,
With every gust, a new jest meant.

Dreamscapes Painted by the Dawn

The sun rises with a giggling grin,
Painting skies where fun begins.
Waves wave back, a friendly cheer,
They flirt with the sand, drawing near.

Seashells gather for morning tea,
Discussing plans for a cup of sea.
A dolphin dances, twirls with glee,
A morning show so wild and free.

Sunbathers stretch, their poses absurd,
Like pretzels twisted, they're lightly heard.
Laughter drifts where dreams take flight,
As ocean whispers greet the light.

With every dawn, a playful tease,
Painting moments with ocean breeze.
In this place where joy is drawn,
Each new day—a laughter spawn.

Where Waves Embrace the Shore

Waves crash with a giggle, oh what a mess,
Crabs doing a dance, what a funny jest.
Seagulls squawk loudly, stealing my chips,
As I laugh so hard, I spill on my lips.

Sandcastles crumbling, a beachside war,
Buckets and shovels, what a chaotic score.
A kid in a pail, wearing a crown,
Looks like a king, but is ready to drown.

Sunburned and sandy, I dive in for fun,
But a wave knocks me back, oh what a run!
Laughing with friends, with drinks in our hands,
Flipping and flopping like fish on the sands.

At dusk we gather, a bonfire glows,
Stories of seagulls and slip-ups expose.
With laughter like thunder, our memories soar,
In this tidal paradise, who could want more?

Serenade of the Sunset Skies

As the sun dips low, oh what a sight,
A painting unfolds, laughter ignites.
A dolphin jumps high, trying to play,
While a fisherman waves, lost in the fray.

Blushing skies whisper, a musical tone,
Caught in the moment, we're never alone.
With ukuleles strumming, off-key yet bold,
The tunes float like foam, stories unfold.

Starfish in dresses, oh what a show,
They tango and twist, putting on flow.
With a splash of surprise, and a giggling friend,
This serenade here, will never quite end.

As waves take their bow, night starts to creep,
We gather our laughter, memories to keep.
Underneath all the stars, fancy and bright,
We're dancing and singing, hearts filled with light.

Gems of the Hidden Coves

In coves so secret, where laughter is found,
Shells tell tales goofy, treasures abound.
A crab wearing glasses, a sight to behold,
Remarkable stories waiting to be told.

Paddling in kayaks, we splash and we spin,
Dodging the seaweed, while trying to win.
A fish-sized balloon floats by with glee,
That silly old fish, thoughts just like me.

Discovery's thrill makes us jump and scream,
What's that in the water? It's just a dream!
With each little find, a prize turns to fun,
Gems in the cove, shining bright in the sun.

As sunsets encroach, the giggles grow loud,
We're united in joy, a hilarious crowd.
Oh, these hidden gems, laughter will thrive,
In the depths of the coast, we feel so alive.

Lost in Lush Green Reverie

In jungles so rich, where monkeys swing high,
Chasing our giggles, they leap through the sky.
Parrots in colors, a riot of hue,
Join in the chorus, no clue what to do.

Leaves tickle faces, we laugh at our plight,
Swatted by bugs, oh what a weird sight!
With vines for our jump ropes, we dance on our feet,
In this verdant chaos, life feels so sweet.

A snap from a branch, a stumble, a trip,
Falling like ducks in a clumsy old flip.
But through all the laughter, the sunlight we chase,
In this lush green dream, we've found our place.

When twilight arrives, fireflies glow,
We share funny tales of our jungle show.
With hearts full of joy, and laughter so free,
Lost in this reverie, you and me.

Coral Castles Underneath

Coral castles, fish in suits,
Building dreams in shell-made roots.
Starfish arguing 'bout the price,
Sandy crabs dancing, oh so nice!

Turtles surf on waves so grand,
Jellyfish swim with a disco band.
Seahorses gossip, sipping tea,
Under seabeds, oh how carefree!

An octopus juggling, what a sight!
Clams chuckle at the silly plight.
Ocean jokes echo through the tide,
Laughing currents, love as our guide.

At dusk the fish wear party hats,
Mermaids join, mixing drinks for chitchats.
In laughter, we find our play,
Underwater all night and day!

A Banyan Tree's Embrace

A banyan tree with arms so wide,
Hiding monkeys, where they glide.
Squirrels gossip, making plans,
While lizards boast of rock-star bands.

At dusk, the shadows start to dance,
Frogs leap in, ready to prance.
Crickets hum a wacky tune,
As fireflies light the world like noon.

Underneath his leafy dome,
Raccoons claim this place as home.
With acorn hats they strut in line,
While the banyan smiles, "This is fine!"

Picnics happen, laughter flows,
Even the breeze joins in the shows.
From lofty branches, echo glee,
In this embrace, we're wild and free!

Dancing Lights on a Midnight Ocean

Dancing lights in waters deep,
Waves are laughing, not a peep.
A dolphin wears a shimmering cape,
As starlight paints a watery shape.

Gulls swoop down, a comedian crew,
Making jokes, just me and you.
With every splash, we giggle more,
As sea foam rises, a playful roar.

Moonbeams twirl on the briny stage,
Nudging fish to join the page.
Sing along with the playful breeze,
While sand dunes shimmy, shake with ease!

Oh what a night, full of cheer,
The ocean whispers, "Come, my dear."
Jump in the fun, let worries float,
In this magic, we'll surely gloat!

Love Letters Beneath the Stars

Love letters float in the night air,
Written by crabs with great care.
Turtle slips one under a shell,
While starfish giggle, "Oh, what the hell!"

The moon writes back in milky flair,
While a wanderer sighs and stares.
Seashells whisper secrets sweet,
As they cuddle beneath our feet.

Frogs croak translations from above,
While jellyfish dance, tangle in love.
In every wave, a story grows,
About warmth beneath bright starlit shows.

So if you see a note drift past,
Know love in the ocean forever lasts.
In waves of laughter we all unite,
Beneath the stars, oh what a sight!

Beneath Arching Palms

Beneath the palms, a crab scurries fast,
Wearing a shell that's a bright yellow cast.
It waves at the tourists with curious flair,
While locals all chuckle, but nobody stares.

A parrot squawks gossip about the sun,
As beachgoers argue about who's the fun.
Flipping their towels with undue delight,
Two sunbathers argue who's tan and who's white.

Each coconut falling, a coconut fight,
Someone gets hit and the laughter ignites.
Seagulls swoop low, claiming snacks on the sand,
While people just wish that they had a hand.

So laughter is carried by waves to the shore,
As each silly moment makes everyone roar.
The sun dips below, casting shadows so long,
And all of us leave—feeling utterly strong.

Serenities of Serpentine Shores

Waves dance in patterns like snakes on the sand,
While surfers debate which wave's truly grand.
The seaweed's a wig for a crab on parade,
He struts like a dancer, with confidence made.

Mermaids and pirates play tag in the tide,
While children build castles in sand that won't hide.
A seagull steals fries right from someone's hand,
And all of the beachgoers just understand.

A sunburned fellow sings off-key as he swims,
While dolphins jump high, turning frowns into grins.
A clam cheers them on, not quite in the game,
But it's happy to watch, and no one feels shame.

Dusk brings a glow to this serpentine spot,
As laughter and stories mingle, a lot.
They pack all their laughter, their memories bright,
And promise to come back again for the night.

Rituals at the Water's Edge

At the water's edge, the ritual begins,
As kids chase the waves, avoiding the fins.
Buckets and shovels are tools for their art,
With castles that topple, they laugh from the start.

A dog takes a plunge, its joy so profound,
Returns with a splash, covering all around.
The owner's exclaim, "That's my best friend!"
While others just giggle, the mess is no end.

A fishing line tangles with seashells' array,
An old man just sighs, "They never obey!"
The fish all conspire, evading the bait,
While seagulls just swoop in and gobble — they're late!

As tide pools collect all the treasures divine,
A crab becomes king, in a kingdom so fine.
With laughter rising high as the sun starts to set,
They promise to return, and no one forgets.

Secrets of the Hidden Tides

The tides bring secrets as night starts to creep,
While mermaids gossip, their giggles so deep.
They trade old sea shells for tales of the sea,
And warn of the octopus, clever and free.

A fisherman sneezes, his nets all awry,
While fish all are plotting a grand escape try.
They bubble with laughter, it's quite the charade,
When his line goes taught, and they laugh in cascade.

The moon shines so bright, like a spotlight on fun,
Casting silver beams, till the night's almost done.
The tides swell with stories, a rhythm to find,
As the sea whispers softly, its magic unlined.

So if you should wander where secrets reside,
Join in the laughter, and let go of pride.
For in every wave, there's a trace of delight,
And the joy of the ocean keeps drumming all night.

www.ingramcontent.com/pod-product-compliance
Lightning Source LLC
Chambersburg PA
CBHW072125070526
44585CB00016B/1553